Chakras

Uncover The Potential Of Chakra Meditation: An Established Method For Alleviating Stress And Attaining Inner Harmony

(The Definitive Manual On Achieving Chakra Equilibrium, Emitting Optimistic Vibes, And Enhancing Aural Resilience)

Nazzareno Molinari

TABLE OF CONTENT

The Seven Chakras - Root, Sacral, Solar Plexus, Heart, Throat, Brow and Crown ... 1

In-Depth Explanation of the Seven Types of Chakras 12

The Origin and Evolution of the Chakras 67

The primary energy centers within the human body" or "The primary focal points of energy within the human body 101

Healing the First Chakra 135

How Chakras Affect Us 166

The Seven Chakras - Root, Sacral, Solar Plexus, Heart, Throat, Brow and Crown

Root

The initial one among the seven is the Root Chakra. The Base Chakra is located at the lowermost part of the vertebral column. The identification of this chakra is established by the crimson hue, which is regarded as the principal spectral color within the visible spectrum. When the Root Chakra is functioning effectively, it will exert influence on the fundamental necessities for survival. These encompass the provisions for accommodating your family, lodging arrangements, sustenance, and the ability to generate income. In the event that it transpires unfavorably, you may incite envy, neglect to acknowledge and embrace your existing possessions, instigate a sense of lack or deprivation and thereby jeopardize the preservation of your assets and circumstances.

One can restore equilibrium to the Root Chakra through the placement of a ruby or garnet gemstone in that area, accompanied by a visualization of infusing the chakra with vibrant, constructive energy that rotates in a clockwise direction. The Root Chakra can also be cleansed by employing black obsidian. Rotate the black obsidian in a counterclockwise manner above the Root chakra, visualizing the expulsion of all the adverse energy from the chakra, swirling away into the stone.

Sacral

The second chakra out of the seven is referred to as the Sacral Chakra. The Sacral Chakra is positioned near the anatomical location of the naval. This chakra is exemplified by the hue of orange. The Sacral Chakra is conducive to heightened states of passion and innovation in individuals. When a society achieves equilibrium, its citizens' inherent artistic inclinations manifest in various forms such as painting, composing, or any other medium of creative expression. When the Sacral Chakra is not in equilibrium, one may experience fluctuating emotions and an inclination to amplify seemingly insignificant matters.

The Sacral Chakra can achieve balance in a manner akin to the balancing of the Root Chakra. When aiming to rejuvenate the Sacral Chakra, it is necessary to employ the utilization of carnelian or tiger's eye gemstone.

Solar Plexus
The Solar Plexus Chakra is the third chakra among the seven. The Solar Plexus Chakra is situated just below the diaphragm and above the abdominal area. This particular chakra is depicted in a vibrant shade of yellow. The Solar Plexus Chakra greatly influences the physical activities you engage in and your overall energy levels. It exerts an additional influence on your actions and the underlying motivations behind them. When a man is in good health, he will cultivate a sense of familiarity with

the physical activities he engages in. They have a propensity to allocate their efforts towards endeavors that are deserving of attention. When the Solar Plexus Chakra is in a state of imbalance, individuals often exhibit excessive preoccupation with certain aspects of their lives. As an illustration, individuals may manifest an inclination toward becoming a diligent laborer. They also have a tendency to make ill-advised choices regarding the optimal approach for ensuring their own survival.

When seeking to achieve equilibrium in the Solar Plexus Chakra, it would be advised to employ the utilization of nectar calcite, golden, or topaz. The Solar Plexus Chakra can be aligned using a similar approach as that of the Root Chakra.

Heart

The anterior aspect of the seventh element corresponds to the Heart Chakra. The Heart Chakra is located at the central region of the chest and is characterized by a green hue. In individuals who have cultivated a deep affection for their fellow human beings, the heart Chakra may radiate a vibrant shade of pink. The Heart Chakra pertains to matters of romance, interpersonal bonds, and above all, it pertains to the emotion of love. In a state of good health, one will cultivate a genuine sense of compassion towards others and acquire the innate ability to express and receive love, as well as effortlessly find companionship. The Heart Chakra also enables the cultivation of self-compassion. When the Heart Chakra is in a state of dysfunction, it can prove challenging to acquire and sustain love and friendships. This could be attributed to the manner in which you have isolated yourself from interpersonal connections during a period when the Heart Chakra is not in a state of well-being.

The equilibrium of the Heart Chakra can be achieved through the incorporation of jade and aventurine gemstones. It should be feasible to restore the Heart Chakra using a similar approach to the one employed for balancing the Root Chakra.

Throat

The Throat Chakra is the chakra that occupies the fifth position among the seven chakras. The Throat Chakra is located at the cervical region and governs effective communication. The Throat Chakra is associated with the hue of blue. When the throat Chakra is in a state of optimal health, one's communicative abilities are heightened, facilitating a clear and receptive understanding of one's thoughts and intentions. This chakra is also considered beneficial for maintaining physical well-being when engaging in public speaking. In the absence of good health, it has the potential to develop into two separate domains of communication. One aspect that can be observed is your tendency to exhibit an excessive dominance in your manner of speaking and engage in verbosity. You often display a modest demeanor, speaking sparingly due to a belief that your words do not carry significant importance.

To restore equilibrium to the Throat Chakra, one can employ blue ribbon agate or turquoise gemstones. The restoration of the Throat Chakra can be achieved using the same methodology employed to restore the Root Chakra.

Brow

The Brow Chakra is represented by the number six out of the total seven chakras. This particular chakra is associated with the third eye, while its hue is indigo. The

Brow Chakra is located in the region between the eyebrows and positioned slightly higher. The Brow Chakra is widely regarded as the seat of intuition, cognitive abilities, and transcendental experiences. When the Brow is in a state of good health, spirituality naturally permeates through you, leading to a sense of self-assurance and inner harmony. When the Brow Chakra is in an unhealthy state, individuals tend to exhibit a withdrawn disposition, disapproval, and challenges with fixation.

To restore equilibrium to the Brow Chakra, one can employ the use of amethyst or lapis lazuli. The Brow Chakra can be harmonized in a similar manner to that of other chakras.

Crown

The final chakra in the sequence of the seven chakras is commonly referred to as the Crown Chakra. The Crown Chakra is located atop the cranium, resembling a regal headdress. The color associated with this particular chakra is violet, occasionally referred to as white. When one is in a state of optimal well-being, there is a profound sense of connectedness to both the world and the vast expanse of the universe. In addition, you effectively manage daily disturbances, effectively devising both short-term and long-term strategies. When the Crown Chakra is in a state of disarray, individuals have a tendency to exhibit impaired decision-making abilities and may experience a sense of alienation from the broader society.

The Crown Chakra can be harmonized through the utilization of amethyst and quartz. Furthermore, it is worth mentioning that quartz can also be employed for the purpose of balancing any of the remaining chakras. The Crown Chakra can be rejuvenated through similar methods as those used for the restoration of other chakras.

In-Depth Explanation of the Seven Types of Chakras

The human body contains several distinct chakras. Indeed, there is a total of seven of them. Now that you have acquired some additional knowledge about the Chakras, we shall proceed to examine each individual type in detail, facilitating a deeper understanding. Consequently, the endeavor to transform your life and experience an unprecedented sense of well-being can be promptly initiated. Furthermore, we will assist you in acquiring a deeper understanding of the various functions they perform within the human body, the consequences that arise when they are imbalanced, and the related phenomena that are linked to their presence.

The Sahasarara, also known as the Crown Chakra, is located at the highest point of the head.

The emblematic representation of a lotus with a multitude of petals, numbering one thousand in total.

The Sahasrara is commonly referred to as the lotus with numerous petals. It pertains to the faculty of cognition and symbolizes the hues of milky white and deep violet. Allegedly, it is believed to foster harmony within the individual and is situated at the pinnacle of the cranium. The chant of the Sahasrara is positioned at the apex of the cranium. This particular Chakra is associated with the individual's emotional states and the harmonious unification of one's inner being. The Chakra exhibits physical dysfunctions that manifest as heightened sensitivity to both light and sound. The psychological challenges associated with the Chakra encompass trustworthiness, indifference, moral principles, and preoccupation with material possessions. When this chakra achieves a harmonious equilibrium, the individual exhibits enhanced intellect, a heightened capacity for open-mindedness and empathy, and a greater aptitude for assimilating diverse streams of information. Lotus is an associated essential oil.

The Sahasarara, or crown chakra, may induce cognitive challenges, diminished focus, and a reduction in empathetic tendencies for an individual. Individuals who lack alignment with this chakra tend to exhibit a sense of superiority towards others coupled with a belief in their own intellectual superiority. Meditation is widely regarded as the preeminent method of chakra healing. Furthermore, the practice of yoga and Tai chi can yield advantageous results, parallel to those achieved through meditation.

Situated at the apex of the cranium, the crown chakra establishes a connection between the central nervous system and the hypothalamus as well as the thalamus. The crown chakra exercises control over various bodily functions, such as the central nervous system, the pineal gland, the cranial region, and the medial area above the ears.

In the event that this chakra's equilibrium is disrupted, it may potentially manifest as enduring fatigue, cognitive impairments, issues with motor skills and coordination, heightened sensitivity to light, psychological disorders, epileptic seizures, ethical quandaries, and a sense of aimlessness.

1 - An Investigation into the Nature and Function of Chakra Energy

Chakra is a term derived from Sanskrit, denoting a rotational or circular object. It refers to a focal point of vital energy present in the human body, exerting influence over numerous functions such as organ operation, immune system response, and emotional regulation. This is due to its capacity to function as a vortex of rotational energy, interacting with a multitude of neurological and physiological systems within the human body.

Every individual chakra resonates at a distinct frequency and is interconnected with a particular bodily area and corresponding organ. It supplies the requisite energy for the proper functioning of our bodies, playing a crucial role in defining our humanity. Additionally, each of them correlates with a specific facet of human conduct and progression.

The human body is comprised of a series of seven primary chakras, with their positioning ranging from the lowermost point of the spine up to the apex of the head. Envision, if you will, a rotational force of vitality wherein the convergence of consciousness and materiality takes place at various junctures along the chakra system. The chakras accumulate vital life force energy, subsequently transforming it, and then transmitting this energy onwards. Prana, the imperceptible vitality, constitutes the fundamental life force that sustains our vitality, well-being, and existence. Our corporal form is inherently reliant on it, while the chakras serve as conduits facilitating the ingress and egress of life force and vitality.

Chakras can manifest as either unimpeded or obstructed. When undergoing unobstructed movement, it reflects their effective operational state. Nevertheless, excessive openness may disrupt the equilibrium of the chakra system. The harmony and well-being of our physical and mental state are influenced by the movement of energy within the chakras. Being cognizant of our chakra system enables us to maintain an equilibrium and an integrated state encompassing the physical, mental, emotional, and spiritual aspects.

There exists a variety of meditation techniques which enable us to achieve equilibrium in our chakra energies by purifying or treating the lower energies, subsequently facilitating their upward ascent to allow for cosmic transmutation of the energy. By constructing an internal realm and cultivating an understanding of our energy sources, we can attain the ability to harmonize our physiological, cognitive, and metaphysical life energies.

The Anahata Chakra:

The fourth chakra is situated at the elevated position of the cardiac region, precisely in the midst of the thoracic cavity. It is the abode of our authentic inner self. The Anahata, also known as the Heart Chakra, is intricately linked to a range of human experiences such as emotions, compassion, love, equilibrium, and overall well-being. It is connected to the thymus gland, which, in addition, forms a component of the endocrine system and plays a crucial role in the immune system, serving as a defender of the body against disease-causing pathogens and stress. It is metaphorically connected to expressions of affection, empathy, and selflessness, serving as a transitional link between the foundational lower chakras (representing primal instincts) and the spiritual upper chakras (symbolizing higher realms). In order to transcend the influence of the ego and tap into a sense of interconnectedness, it is imperative that we navigate our way through the realm of personal emotions. It is at this juncture, situated between the individualistic tendencies and the collective consciousness, that we find the fourth chakra, known as Anahata - the heart chakra symbolizing boundless love.

It is represented by a lotus flower with twelve petals. Anahata is associated with the planet Venus and its elemental affiliation is with copper, which serves as a conductive medium.

The heart center exhibits a direct correlation with the capacity for affection, joy, tranquility, and aesthetic sensitivity in individuals. This realization facilitates attaining a state of balance both in relation to the prevailing circumstances and on a personal level. It has been acknowledged that there exists a process wherein individuals must gradually arouse the energy located within the base of the spinal column and subsequently elevate it to the remaining chakras, consecutively. However, it is worth noting that certain individuals exhibit significantly higher levels of development in their chakras.

The Vishuddhi Chakra, also known as the Throat Chakra:

This denotes the chakra position in close proximity to the throat.

This particular chakra exhibits a significant correlation with the thyroid gland, as well as the organ of action, namely the mouth, thereby attributing significance to the sense of hearing. It aligns with the spectrum of blue light and is associated with interpersonal communication.

It pertains to the inherent expressive and communicative attributes synonymous with human existence. The Vishuda chakra exhibits the characteristic of the spatial domain in which the other four elements are synthesized. Spaciousness is an essential prerequisite for accommodating any object within it. In order to be filled, a vessel must first be emptied; similarly, for what is made evident, the mind must be devoid of any preconceived notions or cluttered thoughts. It is necessary to empty it in order to gain a discerning understanding of the ebb and flow of existence.

The Vishuda chakra exercises control over the vocal cords,

gastrointestinal tract, lungs, and hearing, leading to the emergence of malfunction issues associated with these regions.

The Ajna Chakra, also known as the Third Eye Chakra:

This anatomical feature is located at the frontal region situated between the area above your eyes and the bridge of your nose.

The most crucial facets of this chakra encompass telepathy, clairvoyance, intuition, comprehension of our dreams, and recognition of our fundamental concerns and perspectives on existence. This chakra is bestowed through transcendent experiences that surpass mere physical perception and facilitate a profound connection with the realm of spirituality. It possesses a counterpart within the cranial chakra, situated at the apex of the cranium and holds a connection with the pineal gland. Ajna represents the metaphysical energy center associated with temporal progression, cognition, and luminosity. The pineal gland is an intricate gland that synthesizes the hormone melatonin, which governs the regulatory mechanisms of sleep.

It facilitates the acts of forgiveness and engenders greater comprehension, enabling the contemplation of spiritual consciousness free from the constraints of mental consciousness. Upon the activation of this particular chakra, our comprehension of the profound essence of forgiveness is enhanced, as we gain a deep awareness of the malevolence that incites feelings of animosity towards individuals or circumstances.

At this facility, we exercise control over our thoughts. We can control them. In the midst of silence, tranquility envelops us, enabling us to become keen observers, even amidst bustling crowds or overwhelming challenges. We commence to observe all aspects, thereby identifying the issues associated with numerous inquiries. Prior to addressing the issue at hand, it is imperative that we attain a clear understanding of it. When immersed in a predicament, we experience anger; however, once we distance ourselves, we gain clarity. This is analogous to entering into a state of consciousness devoid of preconceived notions.

Individuals possess the capacity to conceive and materialize entities that lack objective existence. One illustration would be the ability of an artist to conceptualize an abstract notion and subsequently transcribe it onto the medium of canvas. An architect formulates a concept and subsequently proceeds to cultivate the architectural blueprint. By harnessing this ability, we have acquired the knowledge to manipulate our thoughts, construct imaginary structures, and subsequently dismantle them. Such is the extraordinary potential of the intellect, enabling us to traverse diverse realms and transcend numerous boundaries. Nevertheless, we frequently find ourselves caught in this cycle and on numerous occasions we endeavor to liberate ourselves. This type of theatrical performance is commonly referred to as an illusion, also known as "Maya".

The fifth chakra can be defined as the conceptual thought, whereas the sixth chakra entails the perception of visual representations and an awareness of a more expansive life force that encompasses us.

The sixth chakra facilitates an influx of elevated psychic energy, enhanced intellectual discernment, improved memory retention, and heightened determination.

The Seven Chakras: Their Significance within the Human Body and Techniques for Attaining Chakra Alignment

As previously mentioned, it can be stated that the human body consists of a total of seven chakras, all of which are positioned in alignment along the midline of the body. Nevertheless, every chakra represents a distinct purpose and fulfills a distinctive function in regards to our spiritual, emotional, and psychological welfare. Commencing from the caudal region of the spinal column and extending to the cranial or coronal region, each chakra represents a unique energetic force that contributes to our holistic welfare. Prior to delving deeper into the methodologies for aligning and activating your chakras, it is imperative to gain a comprehensive comprehension of the individual functions fulfilled by each of the seven chakras.

The Primary Chakra, also known as the Base Chakra

The Root Chakra, also known as the Base Chakra, is situated at the anatomical foundation of the body, specifically at the coccyx. Referred to as the Kulandini Chakra, this particular chakra serves as the fundamental basis of your physical being, facilitating a deep-rooted connection to the earth. It facilitates a sense of comfort and adaptability in various circumstances, while also promoting an active physical presence. Hence, should your Root Chakra be unobstructed or functioning appropriately, you shall experience a profound sense of stability, rootedness, and strong security across all circumstances. Additionally, you experience a sense of connection with your corporeal form and hold the conviction that you possess an adequate expanse of personal space, regardless of your location.

The root chakra additionally exerts influence over one's immune system, consequently affecting their overall well-being. Moreover, it regulates and governs the various energies within your system, as well as your bodily responses to situations, including the primal fight or flight reactions, instincts, and fundamental impulses. Therefore, it assumes significant importance in determining your responses to various circumstances, particularly when they are novel. This is the chakra responsible for stimulating the flow of energy throughout your body, consequently fostering dynamism, initiative, and vigor in your existence. The impact it exerts on our physical being is of notable magnitude, as evidenced by the correlation between an early occurrence of chakra impairment and persistent daily challenges if left unaddressed. This would impede your progress in advancing through the developmental stage. Therefore, it is of utmost significance in attaining success in the realm of materialism and maintaining commendable qualities such as resilience, fortitude, and forbearance.

Therefore, when the functionality of this chakra is optimal within your physical being, you will experience an abundance of vitality and joy, accompanied by a positive and resolute attitude towards life. Conversely, in the event of significantly diminished energy flow through your root chakra, you will be gripped by a notable decrease in self-assurance and encounter difficulties in effectively fulfilling your commitments within specified deadlines. If your Root Chakra is inactive within your body, you may also experience a sense of being unloved. The Root Chakra, when functioning at a suboptimal level, exerts an adverse impact on one's physical wellbeing, potentially resulting in diminished strength in the lower extremities, compromised skeletal system, impaired kidney function, and compromised integrity of the spinal column.

Consequently, the most effective and convenient approaches to harmonize this chakra involve engaging in culinary activities, attending to household chores, and dwelling close to the earth's surface, whether by sitting or walking barefoot. These actions significantly contribute to the rebalancing of the Root Chakra.

Utilizing Meditation Techniques to Enhance the Balance of Your Chakras

Chakras serve as the intermediary link between the concrete manifestation of imperceptible energy and the interconnectedness of the mind and body. Attending to the various regions of our body will fulfill the requirements of our chakras in order to restore equilibrium, and there exist multiple methodologies through which we may harness the power of meditation to attain this objective.

Contemplation for the Fundamental Chakra

Engaging in the implementation of meditation techniques that foster a connection with the Earth is instrumental in restoring harmony within your chakra system. It is imperative that your meditation exercises center upon harnessing the energy residing within your feet, thereby achieving harmonious equilibrium within your physical being and establishing a grounded sense of security.

One of the meditation techniques involves assuming an upright position, aligning the body, and adjusting the stance by placing the feet shoulder-width apart while gently bending the knees. Maintain equilibrium in your body and gently shift your pelvis forward to achieve an harmonious distribution of your weight across the soles of your feet. Shift your body's center of gravity forward and sustain this posture for a duration of multiple minutes. Indulge in relaxation and engage in the rhythmic repetition of the word "LAM." Employ the technique of breath retention and subsequent release. By the culmination of this meditation, you perceive a sense of assurance and preparedness to embark upon the pursuit of your life's objectives.

Dispute resolution pertaining to the Sacral Chakra

The meditative practice for the Sacral Chakra entails the act of visualizing the extraction of energetic cords originating from the region of this particular chakra within the body, situated below the navel. After severing the connections, it is advisable to smudge the surrounding area with sage. Following this, you should concentrate on the act of clutching a carnelian crystal in your palms, taking three slow and profound inhalations while keeping your eyes shut. Whether in a state of internal reflection or vocalization, kindly express: 'I humbly seek the transcendent essence of purity and affection to establish a connection with my most elevated and lucid being, as well as to liberate any undesired energies. Furthermore, I direct the crystal's influence to restore equilibrium in my Sacral Chakra.' During this process, envision vivid imagery in your conscious thoughts, wherein the hue of orange progressively fills the space of your second chakra, promoting holistic restoration through the administration of harmonized illumination.

Contemplation for the Solar Plexus Energy Center

Your meditation practices ought to center around augmenting your sense of self-assurance. The Solar Plexus Chakra meditation is optimally performed during the early hours of the day. Commence the practice by engaging in deep diaphragmatic respiration while being in a seated position. Envision your upcoming day through mindful meditation, employing deep breathing techniques and attuned awareness of your body. Envision the tasks and responsibilities that require your attention in your daily routine, as well as any pertinent obligations that await you in the foreseeable future. In the event of clear skies, execute this variation of Solar Plexus to allow the radiance to permeate your being, allowing the sun's rays to illuminate your chakra while contemplating strategies for achieving success in your endeavors.

Contemplative Practices Targeting the Anahata Energy Center

There exists a variety of meditation techniques that one can employ to cultivate the Heart Chakra. Assume a kneeling position, maintaining a calm and composed demeanor, while placing your hands precisely at the midpoint of your chest. Quietly repeat the vocalization of the syllable "YAM" whilst contemplating the fourth chakra, known as the Heart Chakra, and its embodiment of love. Continue engaging in this meditation technique until a state of relaxation is attained and a sense of purity and readiness to exemplify love and compassion is achieved.

One: An Overview of the Root Chakra

"One who contemplates upon the radiant brilliance of Muladhara, resembling the brightness emanating from ten suns,

Exercises complete authority over verbal expression.

One reaps the benefits of this vast reservoir of knowledge, perennially basking in optimal physical well-being."

According to Svami, the year was recorded as 1526 CE.

The primary chakra in the system of seven chakras is the Muladhara, which is referred to as the root chakra in English. The term 'mula' signifies the essence or underlying basis, whereas 'adhara' conveys the fundamental support or base. The Muladhara chakra is associated with the fundamental requirements of an individual, encompassing aspects such as personal safety, protection, unwavering support, and the imperative for continued existence. The creature affiliated with the Muladhara is the elephant, an inherently grounded creature. According to perceptions, this particular chakra is situated in the pelvic region, owing to its proximity to the ground when an individual is seated. Bear in mind, it should be noted that the positions of every chakra are not situated in physical locations, as they do not correspond to tangible bodily organs. The locations simply indicate where the concentration of energy associated with each chakra is situated and can be effectively stimulated.

Due to the location of this specific chakra in the pelvic region and the influence of each chakra over an endocrine gland, it can be stated that the control of the Muladhara chakra is vested in the pelvic plexus and the prostate gland. Evidence can be observed in linguistic analysis, as the derivation of the term 'prostate' from the Greek word 'prostates,' denoting 'protector' or 'guardian,' substantiates this claim.

Likewise, the Muladhara serves as the custodian and safeguard of every individual's Kundalini energy. The elemental correlation of the Muladhara chakra is with the earth element. All aspects related to the Muladhara appear to indicate a sense of rootedness and stability, given that it is linked with the color red, which symbolizes blood. According to popular belief, infants are believed to possess a strong

Muladhara since they represent the fundamental essence of life itself. The development of the Muladhara chakra significantly occurs during the initial seven years of one's life, whereby the surrounding environment plays a pivotal role in preserving the vitality of the Muladhara. If the circumstances in which the children find themselves deprive them of the ability to express themselves, or if they possess empathetic qualities and are constantly subjected to the presence of narcissistic individuals who undermine and suppress their opinions, it will result in a pronounced obstruction of the Muladhara. If the child encounters individuals who share similar beliefs and values as they grow older, their perspective will undergo a positive transformation, leading to a restoration of a sense of security and equilibrium within their core energy center, known as the root chakra. The Muladhara holds paramount significance as the primary chakra pertaining to earthly existence, serving as the corporeal vessel of the soul.

The initial trio of chakras encompass the process of familiarizing oneself with the realm of the Earth. They are interconnected with psycho-physical needs. In accordance with the tenets of Hindu philosophy, it is believed that the individual undergoes reincarnation, with the current life being regarded as the initial one being experienced. Each chakra possesses a fundamental sound that enables one to establish a connection and initiate the latent energies residing within the chakra.

The Solar Plexus Chakra

The subsequent focal point in our discussion pertains to the sphere of Willpower and Self-Assurance. The Solar Plexus chakra serves as the wellspring of energy within every individual. It is situated inferiorly to the sternum, approximately at the midpoint of the body. This particular chakra is dedicated to the exploration of one's self-perception and individuality. Fire represents the element designated to Manipura, accompanied by the color yellow as its emblematic symbol. If one is experiencing a deficiency in self-assurance, it may be beneficial to turn towards the Manipura for restoration of well-being.

The Solar Plexus chakra serves as the primary locus for astral experiences, including astral travel, encounters with beings from other realms, and psychic phenomena.

This holds significance for individuals aspiring to embark on an astral expedition, as by cultivating this chakra center, one can endeavor to construct a more potent energetic vessel. Directing your attention towards this chakra may also aid in facilitating smoother transitions during astral projections. A well-balanced solar plexus chakra facilitates the cultivation of robust determination and self-expression, thereby increasing an individual's propensity to explore novel endeavors and establish more challenging objectives. It is an excellent chakra to direct attention towards for individuals who possess a fervor for personal growth and self-actualization. This aspect can also hold significant relevance for individuals struggling with self-acceptance or an incapacity to embrace and appreciate their own identity.

Although possessing self-confidence and a determined spirit are admirable qualities, an excessive abundance of such traits within the Manipura tends to give rise to individuals who exhibit pronounced egotism. Certain individuals may succumb to avarice in their pursuits, whereas others can be characterized as notably self-centered. The potential for individuals to possess a inclination and readiness to exert dominance over others is also contingent upon individual attributes or lifestyles. Conversely, in the event that this particular chakra is insufficiently developed, individuals may encounter feelings of diminished self-worth and a notable absence of assurance. Sensations of insufficiency and subjugation to external influences may gradually overpower your being. The detrimental repercussions may manifest themselves in bodily ailments such as hepatic complications, restlessness, gastrointestinal disorders, and hypersensitivity to certain foods.

To restore equilibrium or enhance the vitality of your Manipura chakra, engage in physical activities focused on strengthening your core muscles while simultaneously fostering a sense of empowerment.

Although it may initially appear peculiar or frivolous, it is crucial to bear in mind that the Solar Plexus chakra primarily revolves around the concepts of self and volition. Consequently, it can be inferred that a mere adjustment in one's cognitive framework possesses the potential to modify the energy dynamics of this particular chakra, as the concept of self is inherently subjective. Additionally, consider incorporating affirmations that promote self-love and acceptance, as these affirmations can effectively revitalize the chakra. Conquering novel obstacles and undertaking responsibilities that demonstrate your efficacy, dependability, and accountability will also promote the growth of your Manipura. Approach each new day with anticipation of its challenges and with a conscious intention to embrace your natural extroversion. In due course, you will find that each passing day presents an array of opportunities and challenges for you to embrace and overcome, thereby reaping the associated gains and accomplishments.

Techniques for Restoring, Harmonizing, and Amplifying Chakra Centers to Maximize Vitality, Happiness, and Serenity

Chakra balancing entails the realignment and harmonization of the energetic flow within the various levels of your being, encompassing the psychic, emotional, and physical aspects. The chakras typically undergo continuous vibratory and rotational movements. Moreover, the oscillations and revolutions they generate have an impact on persistent physical afflictions, glandular functions, bodily proportions, behavioral patterns, and cognitive processes. When an obstruction affects one or possibly multiple chakras, it disrupts the natural flow of energy and creates disharmony. This outcome will give rise to an imbalance, which will manifest itself in the region influenced by the chakra.

Chakras can be restored, harmonized, and augmented through the application of specific methods aimed at elevating your vitality, contentment, and serenity. These techniques encompass Reiki healing, yoga practices, color therapy, aromatherapy, crystal and gemstone balancing, affirmations, fostering positive thoughts, guided visualization, meditation, engaging in physical activity, and employing the emotional freedom technique.

Similar to any other system, if there is an imbalance in any component of the chakra energy system, the overall functionality of the entire system is compromised. For instance, one may consider the gears of a timepiece; in the event that any of the gears lacks proper balance, the entire mechanism will encounter complications, causing the watch to operate suboptimally. This implies that any imbalance in the functioning of your chakras can have a pervasive impact on your overall well-being, encompassing your level of contentment, vitality, and serenity. Consequently, it is imperative to readjust your energy system in order to rejuvenate your state of being.

Color Therapy

The practice of color therapy is alternatively referred to as chromotherapy. It entails the harmonization of the chakras through the utilization of colors. The majority of alternative health practitioners employ this method when addressing specific medical conditions. Color therapy has been categorized as a modality for healing through vibrational energy. Each individual hue within the spectrum possesses a distinct influence over the energetic equilibrium of the chakra system. This can be attributed to the discrepancy in the respective wavelengths of each individual color. The energy emanated by the individual hues of the spectrum corresponds to the primary chakras present within your physical being.

The practice of chromotherapy, also known as color therapy, holds the potential to restore equilibrium to the chakras through the targeted application of suitable hues onto the physical being. There are several simple methods to achieve healing through the utilization of colors:

Utilization of plain-hued textile components.

This represents a cost-effective technique for harmonizing the seven primary chakras, leading to heightened levels of happiness, vitality, and serenity, which can be practiced on a daily basis. Moreover, it is quite convenient, as it can be easily accomplished independently. After obtaining your fabric squares in various hues corresponding to the respective chakras, proceed to:

1. Choose a location where you can establish uninterrupted focus for approximately fifteen to twenty minutes.

2. Recline on a mat, bed, or simply on the floor in a supine position. Please retrieve the collection of seven cloth swatches, each corresponding to the distinct colors associated with the seven primary chakras, namely orange, red, violet, indigo, blue, green, and yellow.

3. Please close your eyes and endeavor to unwind. Inhale deeply and steadily on multiple occasions.

4. As you embark on a state of relaxation, take a moment to contemplate the sequence of events that have transpired throughout the day, beginning from the very last occurrence. Commence from the present moment, retracing your steps in reverse chronological order until the time you awoke, meticulously examining the specifics.

5. Please identify some of the predominant attitudes and emotions exhibited by others towards you, as well as any personal experiences in that regard. Take into account the chakras that

may have been influenced by those emotions and attitudes.

6. Once the evaluation is complete, please proceed to select the corresponding color swatches for the identified chakras and proceed to place them upon the corresponding areas of the body where said chakras are situated.

7. As you maintain your position while the colored swatch lies atop your chakra point, commence the process by envisioning the hue of the swatch being imbued and assimilated through the chakra, permeating into the physical form. Direct your attention towards the act of mentally centering yourself, and acknowledge that while you are in a prone position, there is a process occurring where the chakra

is being balanced. Furthermore, it is crucial to emphasize that the equilibrium of all bodily systems and organs related to the chakra is being prioritized.

8. Inhale deeply while directing your attention towards infusing the color of the cloth swatch into the respective chakra, in order to reinstate equilibrium. Proceed with this procedure for approximately three to five minutes, or until a sense of balance is achieved in the chakra.

Reiterate these procedures for any chakras that you perceive to be in a state of imbalance.

After the successful restoration of optimal chakra alignment, it is now imperative to undertake the process of attaining harmonious equilibrium, enhancing stability, and fortifying their energetic manifestations. "Proceed by executing the subsequent steps:

9. Place each of the seven colored swatches upon their corresponding chakra points located along your body.

10. Inhale deeply and permit your body to effortlessly absorb the vibrant energies emanating from the color samples.

11. Maintaining a reclined position and immersing oneself in the vivid hues, direct your attention to the valuable notion that each of the seven chakras is undergoing a process of equilibrium, synergy, and fortification in conjunction with one another. Witness, perceive, and comprehend that your energetic

system in its entirety is undergoing fortification, subsequently sensing your being harmoniously aligning and comprehending the fact that every facet of your physiological constitution is being restored and harmonized as the hues are assimilated by your chakra centers.

12. Retain the pigmented fabric samples against your person for approximately five to ten minutes until you perceive a complete state of alignment, equilibrium, and energization.

I would also like to suggest the following techniques as equally effective methods of color therapy.

In order to restore balance to an imbalanced chakra, one may choose to adorn themselves with garments that bear the particular hue associated with said chakra. As an example, one may opt to don attire in shades of green when experiencing an imbalance in the heart chakra.

The incorporation of colored lighting in your residence, such as the integration of stained glass or the utilization of light bulbs with varied hues, has the potential to contribute to the harmonization of your chakras as well. There is an alternative approach wherein one may engage in yoga or similar practices aimed at balancing the chakras, conducted within a specifically lit space featuring a colored light bulb corresponding to the intended chakra activation.

Employing organic hues: Another option is to integrate earthy tones within your living space or any location you frequent, which are connected to the disrupted chakra. In the event of an imbalance in your solar plexus chakra, alternative approaches include incorporating plant life, blossoms, or harnessing the natural radiance of sunlight, specifically its yellow spectrum, to permeate your living space.

Illuminate chromatic candles: Ignite a chromatic candle representing the specific chakra you seek to harmonize, followed by engaging in meditation or conducting alternative practices to restore balance to the chakras.

Shall we begin with the examination of the palms of your hands?

The palm of your hands is among the two most influential aspects of your physical being. How?

The Influence of Your Palm in Chinese Medical Palmistry:

According to traditional belief, it is commonly acknowledged that each part of the body is said to correspond to a specific area on the hand. Consequently, by observing the coloration of the palms, one can purportedly detect signs of illness and ascertain various health indicators. Furthermore, according to Chinese medical palmistry, it is asserted that the appropriate method of hand massage has the ability to effectively remedy various ailments within the body. In what manner can we facilitate bodily healing by solely applying pressure to our palms, and what inherent capabilities does the palm possess to perform such remarkable feats?

The Potential of Your Hand in Meditation:

I am confident that you hold a specific mental image of what meditation entails, often involving a seated individual with crossed legs and palms turned upwards, resting their hands on their laps. Our main objective here is to address the rationale underlying the practice of keeping the palm facing upwards. It is commonly believed that this gesture stems from the presence of potent chakras residing within the palms of our hands. By adopting the position of palms facing upwards, one is essentially expressing a desire to receive. What level of authority does your hand possess in making requests and receiving items?

The Influence of the Palm in Islam:

In the Islamic faith, significant importance is attributed to the role of the palms of one's hands in two distinct positions.

During the act of prayer, Muslims adopt the practice of turning their palms upwards while uttering their supplications. Subsequently, upon completion, they proceed to gently wipe their palms across various regions of the body.

During their five prayers, when reciting the phrase "Allahu Akbar" (meaning "God is greater"), individuals of this faith conventionally raise their hands, with the palms facing upwards, in proximity to their heads.

What is the significance of beginning the prayer with the upward-facing palm movement and utilizing it as a means to beseech God?

The Influence of Your Hand in Christianity

Christian worshippers often engage in the act of raising their hands during church services, with the practice being commonly understood as a means of expressing manifestations of happiness and paying homage to

God through the act of worship. This phenomenon serves as a means of establishing a connection with Him, achieved through a simple act of extending one's reach, as if endeavoring to seamlessly unite physical and spiritual sensations. According to biblical accounts, it is said to signify an act of surrender.

Regardless of your religious beliefs, whether you align yourself with atheism, Islam, Christianity, or any other faith, it is important to acknowledge the significant influence that your palm possesses in seeking guidance or energy from a higher power, be it God, Allah, Christ, or even the universe. The process by which your hands possess the capability to serve as a conduit for divine power, thereby facilitating the healing of any other regions of your physique, is a phenomenon that elucidates the rationale behind placing your hands upon your chest and entreating the benevolence of the Divine to restore health to your heart. Doesn't that bear resemblance to the practices observed by reiki masters? Per my previous instructions, continue on the current trajectory while recognizing the potential of your palm and employing it effectively when making requests, thereby enabling the manifestation of your deepest aspirations. Please join me as I demonstrate the intricacies of the healing process, showcasing how it unfolds and manifests.

The Origin and Evolution of the Chakras

Despite the absence of definitive evidence regarding the inception of chakra studies, the substantial influence of Hindus and Buddhists in this realm has resulted in the widespread recognition of chakras as a meditation practice associated with Hinduism and Buddhism on a global scale.

The profound wisdom of these spiritual scholars, who dedicated themselves to the practice of chakras for many generations, enabled the effective transmission of these techniques to subsequent cohorts. They acquired knowledge and provided instruction on uncovering the chakras, as well as harnessing their full potential through the regulation of bodily energy.

In a comparable vein, it is common in present times to encounter a multitude of New Age practitioners who possess the ability to narrate various anecdotes and assert their alignment with the origins of the chakras. Consequently, comprehending the historical origins of the charkas emerges as a significant concern for every student of this methodology.

It is widely acknowledged that the renowned Vedas constitute a collection of ancient scriptures that were documented in India well before the first millennium B.C. Nevertheless, these scriptures were subsequently assembled in written form, with the noble Brahmin families assuming the responsibility of transmitting the knowledge contained within the Vedas to subsequent generations through oral tradition. There exists a supposition that the Brahmins were progeny of the Aryan civilization, which migrated to the Indian subcontinent from the northern mountainous regions.

According to the Brahmin traditions, the concept of chakra encompassed various connotations, with the most notable being linked to the celestial patterns of the diurnal and nocturnal cycles. The Vedas articulate the sun's elegant motion as resembling the chariot wheels of the revered Brahmin rulers, encompassing all that it touches within an enigmatic system of principles governed by time. It bestows cosmic equilibrium and upholds universal harmony.

Curiously, an additional notable reference of the term is found within these ancient texts as a luminous, disk-shaped entity emitting a golden radiance that would manifest preceding the dawn of a new era. This depiction bears a striking resemblance to the divine aura traditionally attributed to Christ in the sacred Christian scriptures.

Simultaneously, it is noted in the ancient texts that the deity Vishnu traversed from celestial realms while clutching four formidable items within his four appendages: namely, a conch shell, a cudgel, a blossoming lotus flower, and a chakra (interpreted by scholars as a disc-shaped weapon).

Additionally, the Upanishads, which were documented several centuries post the Vedas but possess a common origin, contain references to the chakras as extrasensory observers of the conscious being. The Patanjali Yoga Sutras, which were documented approximately in 200 B.C., following a gap of a few centuries after the Upanishads, also delve into this subject matter. Within the Sutras, one can discover the presence of chakras nestled amidst the core tenets of the various traditions, wherein the profound dichotomy between consciousness, encompassing the physical realm and the spiritual realm, is explored.

These teachings alluded to the practice of yoga as a means to surmount the material and worldly desires, and achieve an elevated state of consciousness wherein the human mind is liberated from fluctuations of emotions and caprices. Nevertheless, in light of the fact that yoga is intended to foster unity, it is imperative for the practitioner, known as a yogi, to aspire to reach an elevated state of self-awareness. This entails not only seeking spiritual liberation from worldly desires but also striving to reconnect with one's inherent essence in order to embark upon a novel and loftier purpose.

The depiction of the chakras in the Tantric traditions of the Hindu scriptures has been documented in written records dating back to the period between 500-1000 A.D. These valuable historical texts have subsequently influenced the development of modern philosophical outlooks associated with the New Age movement. The term Tantra was employed to denote a device designed for the elongation of pliable substances. Stated differently, it can be interpreted as a mechanism for cosmic creation that has intricately woven the fabric of Nature, binding it with a solid element while incorporating a contrasting element of softness to complement it.

In Western culture, it has become common to interpret this depiction as a metaphor for sexual duality. However, the original Hindu scriptures present this mystical occurrence as a more expansive philosophical conundrum, illustrating the creation of the universe through the presence of dualistic opposites like good and evil, darkness and light, truth and falsehood, and so forth.

Furthermore, it encompasses the ongoing pursuit of personal enlightenment via the practice of meditation (yoga), adherence to a prescribed regimen of devotional rituals primarily dedicated to Hindu goddesses, and the harmonization of opposing forces in the cosmos to instill equilibrium.

Arthur Avalon was the pioneering Western author to undertake a comprehensive study of the Hindu traditions surrounding the seven Chakras. He hailed from England and his literary offering took the form of a published book in the year 1919, bearing the title "The Serpent Power".

The foundation of his research rest on the contemporary scholarly works of Hindu intellectuals between 1000-1600 A.D. The resultant publication encompasses extensive elucidation on the chakras and offers meticulously crafted practices aimed at comprehending and unleashing their potential. Avalon's work and the sources he utilized have subsequently laid the groundwork for the extensive understanding of Chakras and Yoga in the Western world.

6
The Heart Chakra
Heart Chakra Basics

T

The fourth chakra is anatomically located within the mediastinum, positioned symmetrically amidst the thoracic cavity, in close proximity to the cardiac organ. This particular chakra exercises authority over the spheres of affection and benevolence within our existence. Additionally, it is interconnected with equilibrium, as it occupies a central position within our predominant chakra network, residing amidst three significant chakras positioned above and below it. The Sanskrit term for this chakra is Anahata, denoting "uninjured." This translation serves as a poignant reminder that when our Heart chakra is in a state of equilibrium, we are impervious to the impacts of external factors. The physiological counterparts of this chakra encompass the cardiac region, respiratory system, thymus gland, thoracic cavity, as well as the upper extremities comprising the arms and hands. The fourth chakra is connected to two distinct colors: green and pink. The bija mantra of this entity is Yam, signifying its pronunciation as "yŏm."

A Healthy Heart Chakra
Sustaining optimal functioning of the Heart chakra contributes to the

inherent human pursuit of overall well-being, promoting the attainment of equilibrium, serenity, and genuine authenticity. In an optimal condition, the Heart chakra facilitates the overflow of boundless love and compassion within ourselves, extending outwardly to those in our vicinity.

Heart Chakra Imbalances
In the event of the blockage of the fourth chakra, a sense of solitude and seclusion may ensue. We might experience a disposition towards criticism and judgement, simultaneously exhibiting a deficiency in empathy towards others. On the other hand, an abundance of energy in this context may manifest as feelings of envy, tendencies towards codependence,

or displays of possessiveness. Health conditions such as disturbances in blood pressure and weakened immune responses may manifest as a result of a hindered or hyperactive Heart chakra. Additionally, one may experience tension in the upper back, discomfort in the chest, and potential cardiac conditions.

Five: The Chakra Pertaining to the Throat

The location of our fifth chakra can be found within the region of the throat. It fosters comprehension of the fundamental principles of Universal Laws of Manifestation, empowering us with the ability and insight to adeptly articulate our authentic identities. The Throat

Chakra's energy empowers individuals to vividly envision their aspirations, while bestowing them with the ingenuity and articulation skills to effectively communicate and express these dreams through both spoken and written language. It brings us to a state of harmonious equilibrium between verbal expression and moments of quietude, affording us the capacity to communicate truthfully. The aptitude to proficiently employ verbal and written language is synonymous with transforming thoughts, emotions, and aspirations into tangible outcomes.

An equilibrium within the Throat Chakra provides us with the ability to articulate our thoughts and emotions with utmost sincerity, utilizing language as a bridge to connect with the boundless energy of universal manifestation. As we embark on a journey of self-empowerment through the use of articulate expression, we relinquish our inclination to dominate and govern the lives of others. We articulate our thoughts and feelings comprehensively, yet with prudence and empathy. We cease our efforts in attempting to alter or rectify others, but rather foster an environment where they are encouraged to harness their inherent positive qualities. We commence employing impactful expressions such as I am, I will, I love, and I can, with the intention of motivating ourselves and those around us to actualize our authentic identities and attain our utmost potential. The well-aligned Throat Chakra facilitates proficient communication, unleashing our innate artistic and creative potential. We attain a state of mindfulness and cultivate a feeling of satisfaction.

When there is an obstruction in our Throat Chakra, we encounter difficulties in articulating our thoughts and emotions. We adopt a demeanor characterized by quietness, timidity, and nervousness. Our communication becomes incongruous and untrustworthy, leading us to rely on negative vernacular with diminished impact. The lack of capacity to articulate our thoughts contributes to a state of perplexity concerning our convictions, frequently resulting in an incapacity to harmonize matters of sexuality and religion.

Excessive activation of the Throat Chakra gives rise to the manifestation of self-righteousness. We exhibit tendencies of sexual dominance, excessive verbosity, and addictive behaviors. We steadfastly adhere to our belief systems, displaying a rigid adherence that imposes limitations. We cultivate a sense of apprehension towards authority—an apprehension that external agents or institutions will encroach upon our agency—and this apprehension consequently engenders an incessant inclination to assume control in varied circumstances.

The Throat Chakra exerts an influential impact on our faculties of vocal expression. These are encompassed by the oral cavity, mandible, dentition, pharynx, esophagus, larynx, and cervical vertebrae. It also impacts the thyroid gland, the nervous system, the muscular system, as well as our auditory faculties. Each of these anatomical components enables us to articulate our thoughts and emotions, and when the harmonious circulation of vitality through our Throat Chakra is disrupted, their functionality is adversely impacted.

The establishment of personal authority can be attributed to a well-balanced Throat Chakra. By channeling this energy, we acquire a profound understanding of ourselves and cultivate the capacity to materialize our utmost potential by employing language with creative finesse and eloquence. We attain mastery over our own lives while also aiding others in achieving the same.

The Crown Chakra

This particular Chakra is situated at the utmost pinnacle of the corporeal frame. It is imperative for individuals to channel and cultivate energy in order to attain spiritual enlightenment or establish a profound connection with our spiritual essence. In the practice of meditation, it is crucial to recognize the significance of this particular realm. The flow of energy within this domain enables individuals to transcend mundane concerns and surpass the limitations of physical energy, thereby attaining a connection with their higher essence.

Indicators and Manifestations of Disruption in the Crown Chakra

Physical imbalance encompasses symptoms such as depressive tendencies, heightened sensitivity to light, sound, and the surrounding environment, as well as cognitive challenges impeding the process of acquiring knowledge.

Power dynamics can contribute to emotional instabilities. Inequities arise due to entrenched ideologies pertaining to spirituality and religion, where persistent bewilderment fosters biases and instills a sense of apprehension regarding social exclusion.

An asymmetrical Crown Chakra demonstrates itself through various manifestations. One might find oneself perpetually ensnared in a state of distress, experiencing a pervasive sense of aimlessness, grappling with persistent headaches, contending with melancholy, and encountering difficulties in accessing their inner wisdom.

Strategies for Achieving Equilibrium in Your Crown Chakra

When an individual's Crown Chakra is open and in a state of equilibrium, a profound rapport with their higher power or personal belief system is established. You will achieve a harmonious equilibrium between your conscious and subconscious mind. You shall have the capacity to dwell in the current moment. When the balance of your Crown Chakra is achieved, you will possess the capability to foster empathy towards others.

Meditate Often

The practice of meditation exerts a profound influence on the Crown Chakra, serving as a means of establishing a connection with one's elevated essence.

Envision a radiant golden light permeating your entire crown, encompassing the area immediately above your head. Experience the replenishment of energy, both physically, emotionally, and spiritually, emanating from the glowing aura. This illumination is inherently aligned with your being, serving as the conduit that establishes a profound connection between yourself and the external realm.

Release Your Ego

Ego and self-confidence should not be conflated, as they are distinct concepts. Once you are capable of relinquishing a life that is dictated by your ego, you will commence experiencing a multitude of advantages, one of which includes the considerable improvement of your Crown Chakra's well-being. Frequently, our ego is nurtured by our insecurities, whereas confidence arises from one's understanding of oneself and the capacity to embrace it.

Remain prepared to assist individuals in need.

Make an effort to assist others solely out of your capacity to do so, and you will observe positive effects on your Crown Chakra. Extend a helping hand to others and thereby enhance your bond with your surroundings.

Choose Love

One must prioritize self-love to be capable of loving others. Acquiring self-love paves the way for embracing others. Choose love. Each and every one of your chakras will experience significant advantages, particularly your Crown Chakra.

Prayer

Prayer is inherently personalized, however, it is important not to mistakenly assume that it necessitates a formal demeanor, as that is not the case. Prayer can manifest through acts of devotion or by establishing a focused intention. Kindly close your eyes and allow the inner voice within you to serve as your guiding force.

The Third Eye Chakra

This holds significant importance in shaping the perceptual framework of individuals, influencing their problem-solving approach, their capacity to assess circumstances, and their ability to comprehend and interpret events occurring in the external environment. This particular energy center, commonly referred to as the chakra, affords individuals the capacity to engage in decision-making processes. Such capability assumes significance as these decisions encompass diverse facets of life, necessitating the utilization of faculties such as intuition, rationality, inventiveness, and astuteness.

Envision a scenario wherein this particular part of your physique is obstructed. You would encounter challenges when it comes to decision-making. You might lack a comprehensive understanding and exhibit a pronounced inclination towards biased perspectives when perceiving the world. It is conceivable that you might experience a skewed or disproportionate perspective of the world as well. This would suggest that efforts are required to address this particular aspect within the Chakra system.

What are the ramifications of a blocked Root Chakra?

It is quite expected that you are already aware of the significant role this chakra plays in maintaining your overall well-being and physical health, and that any obstruction in its flow can result in various adverse consequences.

Fatigue is a relatively benign consequence of this type of obstruction, and one that is prevalent in contemporary society given the widespread occurrence of extended work hours coupled with inadequate compensation. In addition, it is possible to encounter symptoms of anemia and a sensation of reduced temperature in the extremities when confronted with this particular obstruction.

Furthermore, apart from manifesting physical symptoms, an obstruction in the Root Chakra can also exert an influence on your psychological well-being. A deficiency in Root energy can result in a state of melancholy. Depression, conversely, can engender sensations of isolation and futility in one's ability to seek effective remedies for their circumstances.

If you have recently been observing any of these effects, it is advisable to contemplate attaining a state of equilibrium in your root chakra energy.

Methods to Resolve an Obstructed Root Chakra

The intricate nature of chakra energy involves multiple layers, and occasionally employing techniques such as utilizing color can significantly enhance one's energy levels. You have the option to attempt these methods consecutively or integrate them together to augment your level of energy, albeit with an additional cost.

Engaging in physical exercise can effectively replenish and rejuvenate the energy associated with the Root Chakra. It is unsurprising that the enhancement of one's physical strength positively affects the Root chakra, which is responsible for regulating the innate instinct for survival. Your exercise regimen does not necessarily have to be excessively demanding.

Engaging in a vigorous stroll or a trip to a fitness center will enhance blood flow and replenish your vitality. Discovering a pastime that brings you pleasure or aligns effortlessly with your daily routine (such as commuting on foot) will facilitate the long-term sustenance of this practice.

The color red is known to evoke a strong connection with the Root Chakra. According to scientific research, it has been demonstrated that the color red has the ability to evoke intense emotions and fervor within individuals, thus corroborating the association with the primary chakra known as the root chakra.

Consuming red-colored foods and beverages such as berries and red meats can serve as an effective means of replenishing your vital energy associated with the roots. The incorporation of a red essential oil in a bath can also be a beneficial remedy.

Meditation is considered one of the most effective methods to concentrate on the chakras individually, giving attention to each specific chakra point in a sequential manner. Try focusing your attention while meditating on the root chakra, if that is where you think you need help.

By directing your attention in this manner, you can additionally discern the origin of the obstruction. By acknowledging your personal challenges, you can proactively confront them using appropriate methods, thereby preventing future hurdles from impeding your progress.

Due to the influence of the Root chakra on one's instinct for survival, it is possible that you have been experiencing a sense of insecurity, perhaps without complete awareness of it. Gaining a deeper comprehension of the genuine cause of the issue can be facilitated through the practice of meditation.

Meditation enables individuals to observe the inner workings of their minds and establish a deep connection with their emotions. Concealing matters from oneself during the practice of meditation can prove to be a challenging endeavor.

The primary energy centers within the human body" or "The primary focal points of energy within the human body

Previously, it has been asserted that the human body harbors seven chakras of immense significance. This presents readers with a comprehensive overview of the chakras, including the corresponding colors attributed to each.

The Root Chakra

This is the primary energy center, situated at the foundation of the spinal column. This chakra holds immense significance and requires continuous equilibrium. This particular energy center of the body facilitates the establishment of meaningful connections with one's family, society, and cultural background. This particular chakra consistently correlates with sensations of pleasure, discomfort, sexuality, and fundamental survival instincts, and is frequently connected to the color red.

The Sacral Chakra
The sacral chakra takes the second position in the sequence and corresponds to the vibrant hue of orange. Located just beneath the belly button, this region correlates

with one's creative faculties and propensity for spontaneity. When one feels prepared to embark on an expedition, it can be inferred with certainty that their sacral chakra has achieved equilibrium. This is connected to your sense of playfulness, emotions, as well as your inner child.

The Solar Plexus
The solar plexus corresponds to the third chakra, perpetually linked with the hue of yellow. This particular chakra initiates at the region of your navel and extends onwards to encompass the entirety of your heart. It is inherently interconnected with one's ego, sense of self-worth, response to criticism, and individuality.

The Heart Chakra

The heart chakra is positioned at the central region of the chest, corresponding to the fourth chakra in the human body. This particular energy center is correspondingly related to the hues of pink and green, and it intertwines with facets of self-assurance, motivation, and self-esteem. It is additionally linked to your affection towards individuals.

The Throat Chakra

This represents the fifth chakra, which is positioned directly at the lower part of one's throat. This particular chakra holds significant importance as it is intricately connected to both your cognitive decision-making processes and your capacity to effectively exert authority when circumstances demand it. One will discover an ample reserve of creativity upon achieving equilibrium in this particular chakra. This chakra is also associated with various forms of energies, among which the expression of truth holds significant value. The color that is linked with this chakra is blue.

The Brow Chakra

The sixth chakra, also known as the brow chakra, is frequently denoted as the third eye chakra and corresponds to the aspect of concentration. The nomenclature assigned to this chakra arises from its location precisely situated between the eyebrows on the forehead. This particular chakra is interconnected with one's sagacity, intellect, comprehension, and innate perceptiveness. The chakra is traditionally linked to the hue of indigo.

The Crown Chakra

The final chakra, known as the crown chakra, resides in the uppermost region of the head. This is akin to the regal crown of a monarch. This particular chakra is linked to the hues of violet and pristine white. This particular chakra remains consistently associated with a transcendent force, facilitating a state of present-mindedness and unwavering commitment towards the pursuit of one's utmost aspirations.

One: Muladhara, the Foundation
Three Stance Exercise

Allocate 5 minutes residing in each of the subsequent postures for introspection, contemplating the sensations that manifest within. What is the sensation of balance experienced in my body when assuming each stance? Among the various positions, which one instills in me the greatest sense of stability and groundedness?

1.) Maintain equilibrium on a singular foot while elevating the other limb to its maximum height.

2.) Execute a lunge by positioning one foot securely in front of the other, while the rear foot is elevated on its toes.

3.) Assume a squatting position, ensuring that both feet are securely grounded and facing the front.

The Grounding Chakra

All stable structures commence with a robust and resilient base. In the absence of this crucial element, the subsequent layers of material would inevitability succumb to collapse and disintegration. The Muladhara, also known as the Root Chakra, bears a striking resemblance to the structural underpinnings of a construction. It constitutes the cornerstone of our Chakra system, serving to establish stability and balance throughout the entire system.

What is the level of significance attributed to a sturdy base? The preceding activity ought to have facilitated the development of an understanding and appreciation for the sensation of stability and established presence. These two elements act as the fundamental framework for the Root. (Incidentally, it can be deduced that assuming the squatting position ought to have provided maximum stability and comfort.) Nevertheless, you may be curious about the precise nature of the Root.

The Root, as its nomenclature implies, represents one's spiritual foundation or essence. Situated at the lowermost point of our spinal column, it serves as the primary energetic focal point in closest proximity to the earth's surface. This is the reason it acquires the appellation Root or Base. A number of the techniques employed to activate this Chakra, akin to the exercise you were instructed to perform earlier, pertain to enhancing stability and embracing the grounded sensation of our feet firmly planted on the earth's surface.

However, the Root Chakra serves a purpose beyond mere generation of a sense of groundedness. In fact, akin to the other six Chakras that will be explored subsequently, the Root Chakra assumes a significant role within our physiological framework. It regulates the fight or flight responses we encounter—the sensations that urge us to either physically defend against perceived harmless threats or escape in the face of danger. Taking this into consideration, it can be deduced that the Root signifies our primal instinct for survival, encompassing our fundamental need for sustenance such as water and food, as well as our fervent pursuit of autonomy and financial self-sufficiency.

Three: The Throat Chakra

After our fundamental needs, societal position, and profound connections have been satisfied, it becomes imperative for us to possess the capacity to express ourselves in order to lead a life that is characterized by well-being and satisfaction. The act of repressing and containing emotions, thoughts, and ideas generates a detrimental impact on our well-being, depleting our mental energy and leading to internal dissatisfaction.

The vishuddha chakra, commonly referred to as the throat chakra, embodies attributes such as determination, knowledge, artistic manifestation, and genuineness

(Olesen, 2014). This chakra places great importance on the concept of truth. It establishes connections with the pharynx, mandible, oral cavity, and thyroid gland. Consequently, when the alignment of the throat chakra is insufficient, it can give rise to discomfort and various ailments within these regions. Depression exhibits a strong correlation with the throat chakra, alongside diminished self-assurance, apprehension, intense distress, diminished artistic or communicative vitality, and instances of aggressive behavior. Deception and lack of integrity additionally restrict the flow of this chakra and amplify numerous afflictions.

This signifies the sacred energy center known as the 'chakra of artistic expression,' which serves as the focal point for creative manifestation. When experiencing a state of underactivity, manifestations such as artist's block and writer's block may occur. An individual whose throat chakra is functioning at a suboptimal level tends to exhibit infrequent verbal communication and may give the impression of being exceedingly meek, reticent, and constrained in their demeanor. Sudden reticence and timidity can occasionally be correlated to this particular chakra. In contrast, an individual exhibiting excessive activity in their throat chakra often engages in a conversational pattern where their speaking outweighs their capacity for active listening. They project an air of being overly moralistic, egotistical, or lacking empathy towards others, often rooted in an underlying apprehension of not being properly understood.

As this particular chakra is associated with veracity and the act of expressing oneself, it is transgressed by falsehoods and deceit, whether they are received by the individual or perpetuated by them. Once an individual is subjected to a persistent stream of deception or indulges in ceaseless dishonesty, they gradually develop doubts about their entitlement to both seek and convey genuine information.

The activation of the throat chakra can be facilitated through the practice of vocalization, incorporating a higher intake of fresh fruits into one's diet, as well as ensuring proper hydration by consuming an adequate amount of water. Directing visualization techniques towards the corresponding shade of blue can additionally aid in unblocking this specific chakra. Envision a luminous, tranquil azure radiance, while simultaneously taking a deep breath, visualizing well-being, restoration, and the calming influence of the color blue. Envision the infusion of this luminosity into your state of health and restoration, subsequently relinquishing stress as you exhale.

Sound is undoubtedly one of the most formidable manifestations of energy on a global scale, intricately intertwined with the resonance of the throat chakra. Engaging in the recitation of positive affirmations, vocalizing through singing, and emitting low-frequency sounds through humming all have the potential to generate vibrational frequencies capable of influencing both your personal well-being and the alignment of your chakras. Engaging in idle talk, disseminating falsehoods, using inappropriate language, reneging on commitments, breaching confidences, exhibiting verbal aggression or harassment, and exhibiting excessive speaking without attentive listening are all behaviors to abstain from in order to preserve the equilibrium of this chakra. Engaging in activities that promote the intentional and effective use of one's vocal cords can contribute to the harmonization of the throat chakra.

The foremost correlation of the throat chakra, in addition to its connection to sound, pertains to the manifestation of creative vitality and individual intention. Your capacity for artistic creation is indeed formidable, and it is inherent within you - even if your portrayal of art is limited to sketching simple figures or you lack the ability to sing melodiously, there exist numerous alternative means of creative expression beyond these conventional activities. Art journaling can serve as a highly effective instrument in facilitating the opening of the throat chakra. This tool is highly beneficial as it possesses the versatility to cater to individuals from various backgrounds, not solely restricted to professionals in the field of arts.

Moreover, it provides a rapid and liberating means to convey one's emotions in a discreet and favorable manner. Art journals can be comprised of photographs, illustrations, drawings, paintings, the inclusion of three-dimensional objects (such as ticket stubs, bubble wrap, etc.), magazine and newspaper clippings, stamps, glitter, stickers, and any other suitable materials one deems appropriate. The objective of the art journal is to relinquish one's inhibitions and unabashedly release one's thoughts and emotions onto the canvas, allowing oneself to freely express in a manner that is personally desired. The aesthetic or logical coherence of it is not necessary; the decision is entirely at your discretion. Embracing this disorder and freeing your manner of expression is crucial to activating the throat chakra.

If the concept of an art journal in any manifestation does not appear compelling to you, the alternative of a written journal is equally potent. The freedom to express oneself in writing without any fear of judgement or the necessity for editing is incredibly liberating in nature. Compose a written account detailing your personal encounters, genuine reflections, confidential matters that may remain undisclosed to others, inner thoughts that one might avoid confronting, emotional states, creative concepts, ongoing occurrences in your existence, past events that have shaped your journey, and any additional subjects of your choosing. Absence of regulations entails that the court is completely under your jurisdiction. After recording your emotions, it is considered a prudent approach to review your thoughts on a subsequent occasion and assess them accordingly. Frequently, this engenders advancements and fresh insights.

Gaining an understanding of one's authentic self and developing the ability to communicate with transparency and candor is of utmost importance in awakening and balancing the throat chakra. Commencing a verbal expression of one's emotions to individuals held dear is frequently regarded as an advantageous initial step. Expressing one's thoughts and emotions may prove to be more challenging than anticipated, notably if the throat chakra remains blocked. However, with steadfast commitment, this feat can be accomplished. After the activation of the throat chakra, individuals commonly acquire the capacity to communicate with transparency, integrity, and authenticity, employing a straightforward manner that proves advantageous to their overall well-being.

1
See the Light

Chakras are energy. Significantly, a vital energy center operates within your body to maintain and regulate its functioning. If one comprehends the mechanism by which the pancreas regulates and reduces the secretion of insulin, a vital hormone for managing blood sugar levels, and comprehends the medical interventions such as insulin injections or oral medication prescribed by physicians to enhance insulin production, then one might grasp the detrimental impact an energy disruption can have on the body. We initiate our exploration with the third chakra owing to its significance within the chakra system. Do not allow the numeral three to deceive you. The Ajna chakra, commonly referred to as the third eye chakra, is closely interconnected with the utmost significance of all the chakras. By acquiring the knowledge of how to initially unfurl this specific chakra and attaining proficiency in its manipulation, you will acquire the essential command imperative for future exploration and activation of each subsequent chakra.

Ajna, in the Sanskrit language, denotes the concept of the third eye, which, when translated into English, is correlated with two distinct words signifying its essence. Command and perceiving. By accessing the Ajna chakra, you stimulate and activate your extrasensory faculties, your reservoir of hidden knowledge, and that inherent higher perception which influences your intuitive discernment, sagacity, and choices. Expanding your awareness to the dormant capabilities that have always resided within you can yield a multitude of advantageous transformations in your life. I will demonstrate to you the methods for maintaining a state of equilibrium, ensuring that the influx of experiences and information does not overpower your senses. Through the assimilation of the meditation exercises that I will offer to you, along with any additional practices that you deem advantageous, you will possess the essential instruments to embark upon this transformative path and activate your third chakra, which corresponds to your intuitive faculty, a latent sense that you seldom employ.

Situated slightly above the level of your eyes, betwixt your brows, lies your third eye chakra in the realm of metaphysics. The pituitary gland and the pineal gland exist within this identical region of the brain. The glands are tightly interconnected with your chakras, wherein one governs numerous physiological processes of the body, while the other exerts influence over a significant portion of the body's vitality.

The chakra system, prevalently mentioned, commences at the sacral region of your vertebral column, specifically with your Root chakra. Located directly beneath your umbilicus lies the Sacral chakra. The Solar Plexus chakra is situated within the abdominal region, while the Heart chakra is located at the central area of the chest. The position that corresponds to the Throat chakra is located at the base of your throat.

Located in the vicinity of your forehead, precisely positioned between your brows, lies the sacred Third Eye chakra, which serves as the primary focal point of our current series. Lastly, the uppermost point of your head corresponds to the Crown chakra. The Sanskrit term for chakras will be employed in conjunction with English terminology, as chakras have their origins rooted in India and its yoga traditions. Acquiring a comprehensive understanding of the historical background pertaining to your field of study can prove to be immensely advantageous, for it enables you to trace the origins of the subject matter.

The forthcoming exercises described pertain to uncomplicated visualization techniques. The human mind possesses immense power; dedicating time to delve into its capacities will undoubtedly leave you astounded. Persevere in the face of delayed outcomes. It is highly probable that they will not be. You simply need to allocate sufficient time and focus towards practicing these techniques, which will yield multiple approaches to strengthening these muscles. You may discover that one approach is more conducive to your imagination, primarily due to the alignment of your inherent talents at the present moment.

When initiating any form of psychic or energy work, it is imperative to engage in the practice of grounding oneself, as it serves as a crucial form of safeguarding. Consider your electrical systems, where each one is equipped with a grounding wire in order to prevent a circuit overload. Similar to how electronic devices require grounding wires, it is essential for you to engage in a grounding exercise prior to commencing your tasks. I can provide you with instruction for a straightforward exercise, and through consistent practice and dedication, you will enhance both your proficiency and strength, just as with any skill that receives diligent effort.

Given the fact that you are performing this exercise for the first time, it is advisable for you to allocate ample time, carefully envision each step, and refrain from stressing about achieving perfection, as it is not deemed mandatory. The utmost significance lies in employing one's intellect to dispel the presence of negativity. That is the sole activity in which you are engaged. In the event that you observe any emergence of negativity in your life, endeavor to reiterate these steps once more. The allotted timeframe is merely an approximation; thus, feel free to allocate as much or as little time as necessary, employing whichever approach you find most suitable and appealing. Once you feel prepared, locate a tranquil and cozy environment, ensure that your mobile device is switched off in order to avoid any disturbance to your focus, and commence.

Establish a Connection with the Earth (Duration of Approximately 3 minutes)

Assume an upright posture within your designated area, maintaining a tall and composed stance.

Envision a radiant, spherical luminosity, resembling a magnetic field, permeating the crown of your head.

Gently guide it across your mind, as it traverses, the magnet diligently attracts any lingering traces of negativity from every nook and cranny, proceeding gradually towards your neck, extracting all the accumulated negative energy residing there.

Direct the sphere of luminosity to traverse your right shoulder, descending along your arm until reaching the very tips of your fingers, subsequently ascending once more, capturing any negative fragments of energy that may have been accumulated within. Proceed gradually to transfer said sphere across your shoulders to the left, guiding it downwards along your left arm and fingertips, before ascending once again.

Harness the luminous white sphere and disperse its radiant essence throughout your dorsal and thoracic regions, allowing each undesirable element to effortlessly merge, thereby liberating your body from tension.

As the sphere descends through your lower extremities, progressively traversing your legs, it dutifully siphons away greater quantities of detrimental energy, instigating a process of relinquishing all pent-up emotions and burdens. As the magnetic force of negative energy, embodied in the form of a white ball, descends upon your feet, you engage in a visualization exercise wherein you envisage the rapid proliferation and expansion of roots traversing into the earth. Through this process, you proceed to expel the aforementioned negative energy via the conduits provided by these roots. The Earth assimilates negative energies from your being, liberating you from the inhibiting forces that impede your progress.

Employing cognitive faculties, direct your roots downward beyond the manifestations of detrimental energy, until you penetrate the nurturing realm of the earth's soil. The roots originating from your core gradually absorb a pristine and ethereal healing energy, ascending through the fertile soil, ultimately reaching the soles of your feet. Now that you have been liberated from negative energies, you effortlessly draw upon the pristine white energy, which gracefully ascends from the soles of your feet, permeating your lower extremities, and progressing towards your thoracic and dorsal regions. From there, it radiates the comforting luminescence of pure white healing light, enveloping your arms and extending across your shoulders, ultimately reaching your neck and enshrouding your head.

Healing the First Chakra

Commonly referred to as the Kundalini, root, or base chakra, the base chakra is commonly associated with fire as well as the symbolic representation of the snake or dragon. It serves as the anatomical and physiological base of the human organism, being located inferiorly to the coccyx and terminally to the vertebral column. The lumbar chakra induces the primordial energy flows within the body, such as those governing digestion, vitality, and appetite, while aiding in the establishment of a sense of rootedness, physicality, and authenticity.

The preeminent aspect linked to the root chakra pertains to the instinctual response known as fight or flight, as it is intimately linked to our fundamental concerns for survival. In the contemporary era, this can likewise be interpreted as our economic stability, concerns or apprehensions pertaining to our domicile, our sense of affiliation, and our bond with our kin.

Glandular system: Adrenal glands
Incense: Cedar wood
Musical note: Middle C
Vocalic sound: U (articulated as you)
Element: Earth or rock
The following gemstones can be observed: Agate, garnet, ruby, bloodstone, jasper, and hematite.
Color: Red

Healing exercises:
Engage in the practice of Kundalini yoga to enhance and activate this

particular chakra and the lower region of the spinal column.

Traversing and gyrating upon the soil without the adornment of footwear. This specific chakra primarily pertains to establishing a sense of rootedness, corporeality, and stability.

Healing foods:

Any items that appear in a shade of red, such as apples, beets, and tomatoes.

Condiments such as tabasco and cayenne!

Earth vegetables and tubers

Beef and protein derived from animals.

Section 3: The Chromatic Spectrum of the Chakras

Color Therapy is highly effective in reinforcing and enhancing chakras due to their strong association with color.

Color Therapy utilizes the seven hues encompassing the spectrum to harmonize and augment the seven vital energy centers embedded within your physical form, referred to as chakras. Color therapy aims to restore equilibrium to energy centers known as chakras, by employing the strategic application of various hues. Indeed, color! The utilization of color therapy has been empirically demonstrated to yield beneficial effects on the physical state of the human body, as well as exert profound influences on the psychological and spiritual realms of the individual. Color therapy can effectively augment the functioning of the body's healing centers, commonly known as Chakras, thereby facilitating the stimulation of our body's inherent healing mechanisms. The complete state of our welfare is not solely a matter of our physical condition. In fact, an increasing number of healthcare professionals are now adopting a comprehensive approach to treat their patients, with an emphasis on the energetic aspects of the body. This phenomenon arises due to the interconnectedness of our body, mind, and spirit, as each element complements and influences the others. Color Therapy is exceedingly beneficial as it comprehensively attends to all facets of our being.

The impact of all our past life experiences continues to resonate with us in the present time. Several of these experiences (and recollections) are favorable, while others are adverse. Over time, the adverse encounters have the potential to materialize into physical manifestations, including chronic diseases such as cancer. Color Therapy has the potential to effectively mitigate these adverse emotions within our bodies, ultimately restoring the body's equilibrium in a positive and conducive manner towards healing. Colors Corresponding to Each Healing Center (Chakra)

VIOLET/PURPLE

The CROWN Chakra, situated atop the head, is influenced by the color Violet/Purple. Violet exemplifies the qualities of beauty, creativity, and inspiration, and has a correlation with cognitive capabilities. Violet is distinguished by the presence of influential leaders and individuals who are devoted to humanitarian efforts, embodying qualities of kindness, justice, selflessness, foresight, creativity, and resilience.

Advantages (PROS) of the color violet

• A profound respect for the sanctity of all living beings
• Displaying a selfless dedication to serving others.
• Idealism
• A capacity to discern the optimal path for the betterment of one's higher being. • A skill in perceiving

the most suitable course for the advancement of the individual's spiritual essence. • An aptitude for identifying the right course of action that serves the greater good of the elevated self. • A talent for recognizing the correct pathway that contributes to the enlightenment and growth of the superior self.

Adverse Implications of the Color Violet

• Lack of consideration for others • Disregard for others' well-being • Absence of empathy for others • Indifference towards others' welfare • Failure to take others into account • Neglect of others' needs • Nonchalance towards others • Disregard for the concerns of others

- Feelings of superiority
- Absence of connection with the objective world
- Disconnection from the realm of reality
- Inability to establish a realistic grasp on one's surroundings

INDIGO

Indigo is responsible for the governance of the Chakra known as the THIRD EYE, which is located in the central region of the forehead. Indigo symbolizes intuitional insights, spiritual discernment, and cognitive awareness, and is associated with the ocular faculties, cerebral region, and nasal passages. The issues that are linked to this healing center encompass migraines, tension headaches, visual impairments, myopia, hyperopia, glaucoma, cataracts, sinusitis, and auditory difficulties. In the realm of personal attributes, indigo individuals typically exhibit characteristics such as intuition, intrepidity, pragmatism, idealism, sagacity, self-accountability, and veracity. Indigo pertains to assuming personal responsibility and having confidence in one's intuition.

Advantages (PROS) of Indigo

- Highly intuitive
- Faithful
- Clear sighted
- Integrity
- Orderly mind

Drawbacks of Indigo

- The lack of confidence in relying on one's intuition
- Scattered mind
- Inconsiderate
- Blinkered vision

BLUE

The blue hue governs the chakra associated with the throat and signifies the qualities of knowledge, health, and decisiveness. The color blue is associated with the respiratory system, particularly the throat and lungs. The issues linked to this therapeutic facility encompass thyroid disorders, anorexia (a multi-chakra affliction), asthma, bronchitis, auditory impairments, tinnitus, upper gastrointestinal problems, oral ulcers, inflamed throats, and tonsillitis. The color blue exhibits attributes such as fidelity, diplomacy, fondness, motivation, ingenuity, prudence, and attentiveness. The color blue is often associated with the essence of one's being, as it pertains to the means by which individuals express themselves, converse, and establish connections with others. The color blue elicits a calming effect on the nervous system.

Advantages and Benefits of the Color Blue

- Loyal
- Trustworthy
- Tactful
- Calm

Disadvantages of the color blue

- Unfaithful
- Untrustworthy
- Self-righteous
- Cold

GREEN

The color green governs the heart chakra, embodying qualities of equilibrium, affection, discipline, and is intricately connected to the heart and breast region. The issues that are linked to this therapeutic facility encompass cardiac ailments, immune system disorders, HIV/AIDS, persistent fatigue syndrome, allergic reactions, and breast carcinoma. In addition, turquoise exerts a beneficial influence on the immune system, while pink is associated with the heart chakra, symbolizing affection and love. In the realm of personal attributes, the color green encompasses qualities such as self-restraint, comprehension, empathy, flexibility, benevolence, modesty, an affinity for nature, and a propensity for romance. The green chakra is associated with the concepts of affection, self-care, and the capacity to demonstrate boundless love and acceptance in one's relationships.

Advantages of Green

- Compassion
- Generosity
- Harmony/balance
- Loving

Adverse Aspects (Disadvantages) of the Color Green

- Indifference
- Jealousy
- Misery
- Bitterness

YELLOW

The SOLAR PLEXUS chakra is governed by the color yellow, symbolizing ATTRIBUTES SUCH AS WISDOM, CLARITY, AND SELF-ESTEEM. It pertains to the organs comprising the liver, spleen, stomach, and small intestine. Difficulties linked to this energy center encompass conditions such as diabetes, pancreatitis, hepatic disorders, gastric ulcers, coeliac disease, and the formation of gallstones. The inherent characteristics associated with the color yellow encompass qualities such as a cheerful disposition, a positive outlook on life, self-assurance, practicality, and intellectual capacity. The color yellow is associated with an inclination towards creativity and an enhanced sense of self-worth, alongside the capability to perceive and comprehend.

Benefits of the Color Yellow:

- Confident
- Alert
- Optimistic
- Good-humored

Drawbacks of the color yellow:

- Feelings of Inferiority
- Over Analytical

- Sarcastic
- Pessimistic

ORANGE

Orange is the color associated with the governance of the SACRAL chakra, positioned in the lower abdomen. It symbolizes joy, self-assurance, and ingenuity. It is associated with the uterine, colonic, prostatic, ovarian, and testicular regions. Issues that are linked to this restorative facility encompass premenstrual syndrome, challenges with menstrual discharge, ailments like uterine fibroids and ovarian cysts, as well as conditions such as irritable bowel syndrome, endometriosis, testicular disease, and prostate disease. The attributes associated with the color orange encompass enthusiasm, joy, and a sociable, energetic, confident, and constructive demeanor. Orange is the shade that is widely linked to achievements, as well as a sense of personal dignity.

FOUR
An International Perspective on the Integration of Yoga and Chakra in Personal Development

Y
Oga is predicated upon physical exercises, yet connotes a holistic state of well-being. Yoga facilitates the circulation of the body's energy and restores equilibrium to the chakras.

The consideration of the mind-body aspect is undertaken, thereby embracing a holistic perspective. Certainly, merely treating a physical ailment without an understanding of its root cause is insufficient. It is imperative to ascertain the underlying reason before contemplating the appropriate course of action. For instance, a headache may originate solely from organic factors such as hormonal imbalances, liver dysfunction, or cervical issues, or it could be intricately tied to psychological factors, such as the patient somatizing anxieties associated with returning to work every Monday morning.

When employing a comprehensive perspective, we acknowledge that an individual encompasses not solely their physicality, but also a multitude of interconnected energy flows.

There are a total of 88,000 chakras present in the human body, serving as pivotal energy centers.

In accordance with ancient Oriental scriptures, it is stated that our physical being is believed to be traversed by 88,000 chakras, which correspond to the specific points where the nervous ganglia and endocrine glands are located.

Energy exchanges and chakras:

Chakras are alternatively referred to as energy centers. They symbolize distinct locations within our physical form where energy transferences occur: internally within our corporeal vessel, between the tangible and spiritual entities, and amidst the internal and external realms.

Chakra: a circular and undulating form.

In the Sanskrit language, the term "chakra" refers to a circular or disc-like entity that serves as a pivotal point for the reception, assimilation, and transmission of crucial life force energy, both within the human body and the external surroundings. It possesses mobility and exhibits a swirling vortex-like motion, varying in speed.

A decline in the energy levels of a chakra aligns with a deceleration of its functionality. Failure to restore the chakra's mobility can result in physical discomfort, while on the other hand, physical discomfort can induce a stagnation of energy within the chakra.

CHAKRA AND PSYCHOANALYSIS

Maryse Choisy and Charles Baudouin can be attributed as the progenitors of the initial juxtapositions between chakra and psychoanalytic information. The second individual is intrigued by the notion of a connection between chakras and specific manifestations of personality, which he discerns by referencing the works of figures such as Freud and Jung, among others. Additionally, he highlights the interconnectedness between the Tantric and Teresian portrayals, specifically regarding the abodes within the "castle of the soul."

A convergence of ideas exists between "Tantrism and Analytical Psychology," wherein individuals practicing analytical psychology, driven by inspiration or the pursuit of meaning in Tantrism, encounter tantrikas (practitioners of tantra) who are similarly inspired by or engaged in the search for meaning in analytical psychology. Several studies have been conducted pertaining to the phenomena of kundalini awakening, chakra activation, and related subjects.

CHAKRA AND BUDDHISM

The tantric Hindu models, along with certain modifications, were incorporated into the practices of Buddhist Tibetan and Shingon Japanese traditions, specifically the Vajrayāna system. Within these traditions, there exists a concept of five centers which correspond to the five elements and five Buddhas, often referred to as the Dhyanis, and are commonly described as nine. In a broader context, within the realm of Buddhism, the wheel also serves as an emblem to represent the Buddha, the Dharma, and concepts pertaining to authority.

In Buddhist iconography, the chakra also refers to the luminous aura encircling the heads of holy individuals, known as the shirashchakra. Additionally, it encompasses the radiant emanation surrounding their bodies, commonly referred to as the prabhâvali, which manifests as a fiery composition of flames, aptly known as the jvâla.

Prior to the convergence of the Indian and Greek civilizations, the depiction of the Buddha solely relied on a symbolic wheel, occasionally positioned atop a pillar or elevated structure, similar to the capital of Ashoka which subsequently became synonymous with India.

1: Insights Provided by the Ascended Masters

Everything is in rhythm. When our actions align with the harmonious cadence of the cosmos, adversities do not ensue. The rhythm is comprised of both masculine and feminine forces, and the division of these energies generates an inequity and annihilation.

The rhythm is commonly known as the Dance of Nataraj in the realm of Hindu philosophy. The arrangement of natural elements displays a rhythmic pattern. Energy is constantly being exchanged, with the conversion of energy into mass and vice versa being described by the equation $E=mc^2$. Hence, in accordance with the principles of quantum physics, we possess the capacity to alter our predetermined trajectory. We possess ultimate control over our own destiny. Regrettably, we make choices in accordance with the outcomes predetermined by our karmic actions.

Each occurrence in life presents an opportunity to acquire knowledge and wisdom. In life, every occurrence is not without intent; rather, we shape our reality based on what we nurture in our consciousness. The entirety of existence resides within the realm of the human psyche. Upon gaining knowledge of the intricacies of the human psyche, the mind assumes the capacity to either serve as our staunchest ally or our most formidable adversary, contingent upon our diligence in pursuit of veracity.

When we lack resonance with the metaphysical interconnectedness enveloping our existence, we experience anguish. We embody a holographic representation of the universe on both microscopic and macroscopic scales. This concept is elaborated upon in the ancient Sanskrit literary narrative known as the 'Tripura Rahasya', which unfolds the enigma that extends beyond the concept of a trinity.

Through the practice of meditation under the instruction of an enlightened mentor, one can experience the dissolution of impurities and the cessation of all adverse reactions. Those individuals who desire to attain freedom from illnesses ought to direct their external awareness inward. The intellect perceives a sense of reality when it engages with the stimuli received through the five sensory faculties. When one gains the capacity to employ the sixth sense, they bear witness to the ultimate verity.

Our cellular structures experience a perpetual cycle of decay and renewal. Over the course of one year, the cells within the body undergo a process of rejuvenation.

Scholars delineate illnesses as disruptions in tranquility.

Quantum physics reveal:
• Emotions represent the dynamic expression of energy. Emotions arise as a result of psychic imprints, where these imprints are imprinted onto the cognitive faculty, giving rise to thoughts, and ultimately shaping the perception of reality. Ideas are generated by the cognitive faculty, and the cognitive faculty is shaped by one's actions.

• Emotions give rise to somber accumulations, which manifest as physical maladies.

•Physical pain serves as an outward expression of guilt, stemming from either one's current actions or previous experiences in life.

• Cancer arises in individuals who harbor profound resentments, when their ability to respond to oppression is compromised; these individuals' emotional states generate vibrations that consequently give rise to atomic arrangements that lead to the formation of cancerous cells.

• The presence of perpetual fear contributes to the development of asthma.

•Emotions characterized by a sense of powerlessness and subjugation can result in physical symptoms such as weakened leg muscles and knee disorders.

•Unresolved tasks emit a colorless energy that transforms into a vibrant golden energy once they are finished.

• The implementation of respiratory regulation facilitates the management of one's entire existence.

How Chakras Affect Us

An apt analogy to consider in relation to chakras is to regard them as the energetic equivalent of the digestive system. Chakras receive energy, undergo processing, and subsequently eliminate any necessary contents. Individuals possess significant levels of energy. Irrespective of one's awareness, the human body consistently experiences a perpetual influx and efflux of energy. When an individual maintains the clarity, stability, and safeguarding of their personal energy, they can be assured that the energy they subsequently extend to others is steadfastly pristine.

Should an individual succumb to the influence of their detrimental thoughts, perspectives, or convictions, regrettably, this negativity shall inevitably permeate their interactions with others. The aforementioned statement also applies in case you encounter an adverse energetic manifestation originating from another person. You will subsequently be influenced, in a manner of speaking, by the adverse energy emanating from this individual. The negative energy will undergo absorption by your chakras, subsequently necessitating increased efforts by your chakras to restore equilibrium and eliminate said negative energy.

If an individual's chakras are consistently subjected to unfavorable or burdensome energy, whether due to the negativity of others or their own internal negativity, the chakras will become overburdened as they remain in a perpetual state of contamination. Excessive workload can lead to a decrease in the flow and vitality of one's chakras, causing them to become stagnant, impure, and obstructed. In the event of such occurrences, it will be imperative to undertake a comprehensive revitalization process to ensure their optimal functioning is reinstated.

The term "Chakra" signifies a "rotating apparatus," thus evoking the image of a substantial, energetic wheel in motion. It efficiently draws in the energy, creates rotational motion to effectively distinguish between necessary and unnecessary elements, and subsequently redistributes it beyond the physical confines of the organism. Given our inherent vitality and the role chakras play in balancing our energies, it becomes evident that they wield significant influence over us. Should our chakras be contaminated, obstructed, or excessively strained, their impact on our state of mind would essentially confine us to a perpetual state of negativity, typically manifested as anger and depression. The chakras exert a profound influence on our mental state, as a deficiency in our energy manifests as pessimistic thoughts, while an abundance of positive energy fosters optimistic thinking. This phenomenon occurs due to the inadequate strength or obstruction of our chakras, rendering them incapable of purging negative energy and assimilating positive energy.

Our spiritual well-being is intertwined with the functioning of our chakras. As previously discussed, the state of our energy greatly influences our ability to emanate and manifest positive energies towards those in our vicinity. Nevertheless, if our energy is filled with negativity, it possesses the capability to permeate and influence those in our vicinity. This is a profoundly lamentable and occasionally perilous incident. Ultimately, it is of utmost importance to ensure that we do not transmit periods of anger and depression to others under any circumstances, should there be any measures available to avoid such transmission. Hence, the maintenance of one's personal chakras in a state of equilibrium holds significant importance. Later in this book, we shall provide an in-depth examination of the techniques involved in restoring balance to your chakras, indicators that may suggest an existing imbalance, and strategies to rectify such imbalances.

There is a widely held belief that the chakras possess the ability to influence various aspects of the physical body. It has been widely reported that the number of chakras is believed to exceed one hundred, however, only seven essential, or principal, chakras are commonly acknowledged. These chakras will be further elaborated upon in the subsequent .

The impact on your physical well-being is contingent upon the precise positioning and condition of the chakra in consideration. In the event of a chakra obstruction or malfunction, one may experience discernible physiological manifestations. As an illustration, should an issue arise with the chakra located in your throat, the absence of resolution may give rise to a physical manifestation, such as the onset of a common cold, a persistent cough, or, in more severe instances, the formation of a palpable lump. The throat chakra may become influenced when individuals contemplate expressing themselves to others, but subsequently deter themselves from doing so, resulting in the suppression of their thoughts and emotions. One may perceive this sensation as a constriction in the throat, reminiscent of the discomfort experienced during attempts to hold back tears. Subsequently, if the unresolved imbalances within the throat chakra persist, tangible physical manifestations may ensue. The likelihood of alleviating these effects rests upon the articulation of one's thoughts and needs to the relevant individual.

There is a myriad of ways in which chakras can impact our physical well-being, and the aforementioned instance merely represents but a single illustration. It is widely acknowledged that an intricate network of chakras pervades the entirety of the human physique, bridging together various facets that constitute an individual, including the cognitive, emotional, spiritual, and physiological dimensions, revealing their profound interconnectedness.

Methods for Achieving Chakra Equilibrium, Restoration, and Purification to Cultivate Vibrant Energy

Are you aware of the abundance of energy present within your physical being? I am referring to a different type of energy, distinct from the energy derived from the consumption of food. I am alluding to the energy that is emitted during its interaction with the surrounding environment. By doing so, it emits this vital energy (referred to as prana) as a rotational mechanism where substance and awareness converge to maintain our well-being, vitality, and existence. This rotating wheel aligns with the primary neural centers within your physique.

These primary centers of neural activity align with the positioning of the seven chakras, as well as the vital organs, while also influencing our spiritual, emotional, and psychological well-being. In light of the perpetual motion of all things, it is imperative that the seven primary chakras remain open, correctly aligned, and fluid in order to prevent any obstruction that could impede the flow of energy.

This situation is analogous to that of a bathtub, where the accumulation of excess hair in the drain leads to a blockage, impeding the flow of water. Consequently, the stagnant water fosters the growth of bacteria and mold. The aforementioned scenario applies to the chakras as well; however, unlike bathtubs, which can be easily unclogged, the task of unclogging, activating, or harmonizing the chakras poses a formidable challenge.

The process of harmonizing your chakras entails realigning the energy flow within your body on multiple planes, encompassing the physical, emotional, and psychic realms. The perpetual rotation and vibration of your chakras perpetually exert a discernible impact on intricate aspects of your being, such as glandular functions, bodily afflictions, behavioral patterns, bodily form, and cognitive thought processes. Should any aspect of the energetic systems within your chakras become compromised, the overall functioning of your entire system will be inhibited. If an imbalance occurs in one or more chakras, it will have a pervasive impact on your entire system, leading to a disruption in its optimal functioning. This will impact your emotional state, potentially disrupting feelings of happiness and serenity until equilibrium is restored.

The equilibrium and restoration of your chakras can be achieved through the utilization of various methodologies, resulting in the manifestation of vibrant vitality within you. The methodologies encompass color therapy, yoga, Reiki healing, aromatherapy, affirmations, guided visualization, utilization of gemstones and crystals, physical exertion, and a plethora of additional practices.

Following are a few methods for achieving equilibrium, restoration, and purification of your chakras.

Techniques of Mudras and Mantras for Chakra Balancing

The term "Mudra" originates from the Sanskrit language, denoting the concepts of "sign" or "seal." This is an action or hand posture employed to manipulate and direct the flow of energy, effectively stimulating cognitive processes. This concept can be understood as mudras serving as conduits to facilitate the activation of chakras, thereby enabling the channeling of heightened energy towards targeted chakras in order to attain the desired state of equilibrium. In order to augment the efficacy of mudras, vocalizations of Sanskrit syllables are intoned. When uttered, they elicit a vibratory effect within your physique, which engenders a tangible sensation at the corresponding chakra.

How To Do Mudras

Through the act of tactile manipulation, involving touching, stretching, crossing, or curling the hands and fingers, one possesses the ability to effectively communicate with both the physical and mental aspects of the self. It is widely held that distinct regions of the hand are intricately linked to specific regions of the mind or body, allowing for a meaningful interaction between the two. In due course within the designated , we shall elaborate on the correlation between each of your digits and the five fundamental elements: earth, metal, fire, wood, and water, commencing from the pinky finger and progressing towards the thumb.

Rest your hands on your lap with your palms facing upwards and overlapping, ensuring that your left hand is positioned underneath the right hand's palm and gently touching the back of the fingers. Please ensure that you lightly bring the tips of your thumbs together, directing your attention towards the sacral chakra, before proceeding to intone the syllable VAM. By engaging in this practice, you will activate and restore balance to your sacral chakra.

Mudras can be practiced in any location without prior arrangements, and they can be performed with discretion. As previously stated, it can be observed that your fingers exhibit a correspondence to not only the five elements, but also to emotions and the primary organs within the human body. The meridians traverse both the external and internal aspects of your fingers, rather than the superior and inferior regions. Through applying pressure or gentle compression to the lateral aspects of the fingers, in accordance with your specific requirements, it is possible to exert influence on both the associated emotion and the corresponding organ. The following elucidates the functioning of the fingers:

The thumb symbolizes the earthly element, the stomach, and a sense of apprehension.

The index finger typically symbolizes the metallic element and exhibits a strong correlation with emotions such as sorrow, melancholy, and desolation, as well as the functions of the large intestines and the lungs.

The middle finger symbolizes the element of fire and is commonly associated with the respiratory and circulatory systems, emotional traits such as impulsiveness and restlessness, as well as the small intestines and the heart.

The fourth finger, also known as the ring finger, correspondingly represents the element of wood and exhibits a strong connection to emotions of anger, the nervous system, the gall bladder, and the liver.

With regards to the pinky finger, it symbolizes the element of water and exhibits a strong association with fear and the renal system.

Whenever an individual experiences a sense of emotional overwhelm, they merely need to apply slight pressure to the corresponding digit in order to alleviate their distress. Moreover, in the case where a particular finger corresponds to a specific organ linked to a particular chakra, one may also apply pressure to that specific finger for therapeutic purposes. It is fairly straightforward, correct?

www.ingramcontent.com/pod-product-compliance
Lightning Source LLC
Chambersburg PA
CBHW050413120526
44590CB00015B/1949